THE ULTIMATE GUIDE TO

BILLIE
EILISH

100% UNOFFICIAL

A STUDIO PRESS BOOK

First published in the UK in 2020 by Studio Press,
an imprint of Bonnier Books UK,
The Plaza, 535 King's Road, London SW10 0SZ

www.studiopressbooks.co.uk
www.bonnierbooks.co.uk

© 2020 Studio Press Books

1 3 5 7 9 10 8 6 4 2

ISBN 978-1-78741-836-3

Written by Dan Whitehead and Daizy Whitehead
Edited by Sophia Akhtar
Designed by Wendy Bartlet

All images © Shutterstock, Alamy and Getty Images

A CIP catalogue for this book is available from the British Library
Printed and bound in Poland

THE ULTIMATE GUIDE TO

BILLIE EILISH

100% UNOFFICIAL

CONTENTS

FACT FILE

FULL NAME	Billie Eilish Pirate Baird O'Connell
BIRTHDAY	18 December 2001
HEIGHT	5 ft 4 in, or 162 cm
NATURAL HAIR COLOUR	Blonde
STAR SIGN	Sagittarius
BIRTH PLACE	Los Angeles, California
PARENTS	Maggie Baird and Patrick O'Connell
SIBLINGS	Finneas O'Connell
BELIEFS	Vegan
PHOBIAS	Deep water and the dark
CAR	Dodge Challenger named 'Dragon'

BILLIE STILL LIVES AT HOME WITH HER PARENTS IN THEIR 100-YEAR-OLD TWO-BEDROOM HOUSE. HER MUM AND DAD USED TO SLEEP IN THE LIVING ROOM TO MAKE SPACE FOR FINNEAS AND BILLIE'S RECORDING STUDIO!

Over 56 million Instagram followers!

Over 27 million YouTube subscribers!

Over 15 billion Spotify streams!

Over 5.5 billion YouTube views!

Billie shares her birthday with film director Steven Spielberg, actor Brad Pitt and singer Christina Aguilera.

Billie's mum won't let her drink fizzy soft drinks, like Coke or Pepsi!

Some of Billie's old Instagram usernames are @wherearetheavocados, @riderofthewind, @disasterpiece and @dead.cow!

BILLIE EILISH

HER STORY SO FAR...

EVEN THOUGH SHE'S STILL A TEENAGER, BILLIE HAS CRAMMED A LOT INTO HER LIFE ALREADY! YOU COULD SAY THAT PERFORMANCE AND CREATIVITY ARE IN HER BLOOD, AS SHE WAS BORN IN DECEMBER 2001 TO MAGGIE BAIRD AND PATRICK O'CONNELL, BOTH KEEN MUSICIANS AND ACTORS. HER OLDER BROTHER, FINNEAS, WAS BORN FOUR YEARS EARLIER IN 1997.

The family has strong Irish and Scottish roots, which is where Billie's name comes from. Her full name is Billie Eilish Pirate Baird O'Connell. In an interview with the BBC in 2017, she joked about her unusual name:

'Pretty weird, right? Pirate was going to be my middle name but then my uncle had a problem with it because pirates are bad.'

In actual fact, it was Finneas – then aged four – who wanted to call her **Pirate!** Her parents wanted to call her Eilish, after seeing a documentary about Irish conjoined twins with the name. In the end, though, they ended up choosing Billie as her first name, in honour of her grandfather, Bill, who died before she was born.

GROWING UP

IN THE
O'CONNELL
FAMILY

AS A CHILD, BILLIE GREW UP IN THE LOS ANGELES NEIGHBOURHOOD OF HIGHLAND PARK, ONE OF THE CITY'S OLDEST AREAS. IT'S FILLED WITH TRENDY RECORD SHOPS AND VINTAGE CLOTHING STORES, AND HOME TO LOADS OF ARTISTIC COMMUNITIES, TECHNOLOGY COMPANIES AND MUSIC LABELS.

It wasn't always like that, though. 'Highland Park has become popular now but growing up there, it was not like that at all,' she told *NME*. 'There were gunshots, y'know – it was really sketchy. People just have a different vision of how I was raised and that's not correct. They think I'm just a little rich girl from LA.'

> **'There were gunshots, y'know — it was really sketchy.'**

Both Billie's parents play lots of different musical instruments, and they decided that they would teach their children themselves, at home, rather than send them to a traditional school. This meant that Billie and Finneas were encouraged to pursue their creative dreams without having to worry about tests and exams. Sounds pretty amazing, right?

'Homeschooling allows us to let them do the things that they really love to do and not have a giant academic schedule on top of it,' Billie's mother told *Your Teen* magazine.

It's no surprise that Billie was writing songs before most kids can even write their name. She even recorded herself singing some of them, including one about falling into a black hole, which she wrote at the age of just four years old! 'It was really upbeat,' she recalled in an interview in 2017. 'Like, 'I'm going down, down, down, into the black hole. It went on and on.'

ALL-SINGING, ALL-DANCING

BY THE AGE OF EIGHT, BILLIE WAS TAKING PART IN TALENT SHOWS AND HAD JOINED THE LOS ANGELES CHILDREN'S CHORUS, A FAMOUS CHOIR GROUP, WHICH PERFORMED AT LEGENDARY VENUES LIKE THE HOLLYWOOD BOWL. SHE CREDITS THE CHOIR WITH TEACHING HER HOW TO PROTECT HER VOICE AND USE PROFESSIONAL VOCAL TECHNIQUES.

'Some artists just ruin their voices because they don't know any better,' she says.

Aged 11, Billie wrote what she considers to be her first proper song for an assignment in her mother's songwriting class. It was called *Fingers Crossed* and was a love song set during a zombie apocalypse! 'The assignment was to watch a movie or a show and write down certain lines that you thought were good hooks, good titles or good names,' she says. 'And I watched *The Walking Dead*, because that was my favourite show at the time, and I got tons of stuff.'

As well as singing, Billie was also taking part in a competitive dance group, an experience that would change her life in more ways than one. She hated the tight clothing dancers had to wear and, faced with a close-knit clique of confident popular girls, Billie's confidence plummeted.

'That was probably when I was the most insecure,' she later told *Rolling Stone* magazine. 'I wasn't as confident. I couldn't speak and just be normal. When I think about it or see pictures of me then, I was so not OK with who I was.'

OCEAN EYES

Despite this, Billie's skill shone through, and she was assigned to the most advanced classes. One of her dance teachers heard her humming a song and suggested she record it so she'd have something original to choreograph a dance routine to. That song was *ocean eyes* written by Finneas for his band, but her generous brother agreed that Billie's version sounded better, and they should record it together.

Then disaster struck. Only a few days after recording *ocean eyes* and starting to work out a dance routine for it, Billie suffered a terrible injury during one of her classes, rupturing the growth plate where her leg joins the hip. This agonising accident meant she had to stop dancing immediately. At the age of 13, it seemed like Billie's dreams were over before they'd even begun.

> **We were like, what the hell is going on?**

Meanwhile, *ocean eyes* was sitting there online. Neither Billie nor Finneas expected anyone else to listen to the song. They'd uploaded a few songs to Soundcloud before, for their friends to hear, and only uploaded *ocean eyes* so her dance teacher could download it to use in class! Instead, it started to go viral, spreading from friends to strangers, until eventually producers, DJs and music websites were playing it and recommending it to people. Before long, the track had been listened to hundreds of thousands of times. Looking back on her sudden success, Billie said: 'I would hit refresh and it would have a bunch of new plays. We were like, what the hell is going on?'

IN MARCH 2016 BILLIE SHOT A MUSIC VIDEO TO ACCOMPANY THE SONG AND THINGS HAPPENED INCREDIBLY QUICKLY ONCE THE MUSIC INDUSTRY KNEW THERE WAS A TALENTED TEENAGER GETTING MILLIONS OF SOUNDCLOUD HITS. BY AUGUST SHE WAS SIGNED UP BY INTERSCOPE, A LABEL THAT IS ALSO HOME TO LANA DEL REY, LADY GAGA AND EMINEM, AND *OCEAN EYES* WAS RELEASED AS AN OFFICIAL SINGLE IN NOVEMBER.

The manager of Finneas's band hooked her up with a publicist, who brought her to the attention of fashion label Chanel. And all the time, that listener count on *ocean eyes* kept getting higher and higher.

FAME

Billie's life became a whirlwind of new music releases and promotional shows. She started 2017 as a quirky newcomer and ended the year as one of the most praised and popular stars on the planet, with a string of hit singles! In the space 12 months she went from playing to small crowds in tiny clubs to headlining famous venues filled with thousands of fans. Selena Gomez picked Billie's song *Bored* to feature on the soundtrack to the hit Netflix series *13 Reasons Why*, and established hip hop stars, such as Vince Staples and Khalid, lined up to work with her and remix her tracks.

Fast forward to the end of 2019 and the girl who recorded weird pop songs in her bedroom with her brother had broken world records, earned loads of major awards and been asked to record the theme song for a massive blockbuster movie. She's accomplished more as a teenager than most artists manage in their entire lives — wherever she goes next in 2020 and beyond, it's sure to be amazing!

TIMELINE

DECEMBER 2001

BILLIE EILISH PIRATE BAIRD O'CONNELL WAS BORN IN LOS ANGELES ON 18TH DECEMBER. MERRY CHRISTMAS!

2009

BILLIE JOINS THE LOS ANGELES CHILDREN'S CHORUS.

NOVEMBER 2016

BILLIE SIGNS A RECORD DEAL. *OCEAN EYES* BECOMES A WORLDWIDE HIT.

AUGUST 2017

BILLIE RELEASES THE *DON'T SMILE AT ME* EP IN AUGUST.

BILLIE WRITES HER FIRST SONG AT THE AGE OF FOUR.

2005

BILLIE UPLOADS *OCEAN EYES* TO SOUNDCLOUD IN NOVEMBER. IT GETS MILLIONS OF VIEWS.

NOVEMBER 2015

BILLIE RELEASES FOUR SINGLES: *BELLYACHE*, *BORED*, , *WATCH* AND *COPYCAT*.

2017

BILLIE SETS OFF ON HER *WHERE'S MY MIND* TOUR, PLAYING IN BRITAIN, EUROPE AND ACROSS THE UNITED STATES.

FEBRUARY 2018

MARCH 2019

HER FIRST FULL-LENGTH ALBUM, *WHEN WE ALL FALL ASLEEP, WHERE DO WE GO?*, DROPS IN MARCH. IT IS AN INSTANT SMASH!

2020

BILLIE PERFORMS *NO TIME TO DIE* LIVE AT THE BRIT AWARDS.

APRIL 2018

IN APRIL BILLIE RELEASES *LOVELY*, A COLLABORATION WITH KHALID. IT FEATURES ON THE SOUNDTRACK TO *13 REASONS WHY*.

2020

BILLIE WINS FIVE GRAMMY AWARDS, INCLUDING ALBUM OF THE YEAR.

BILLIE RELEASES HER SIXTH SOLO SINGLE, *WHEN THE PARTY'S OVER*, IN OCTOBER.

BILLIE MAKES HER FIRST EVER MUSIC FESTIVAL APPEARANCES AT COACHELLA IN APRIL AND GLASTONBURY IN JUNE, PLAYING TO MASSIVE CROWDS.

OCTOBER 2018

BILLIE RELEASES TWO MORE SINGLES, *BURY A FRIEND* AND *WISH YOU WERE GAY*.

2019

BILLIE IS ANNOUNCED AS THE SINGER OF THE THEME SONG FOR THE JAMES BOND MOVIE, *NO TIME TO DIE*.

2019

2020

SAY HELLO TO

BILLIE ISN'T THE ONLY TALENTED ONE IN HER FAMILY. SHE COMES FROM A WHOLE HOUSE FULL OF ACTORS AND MUSICIANS!

* Billie's mother is Maggie Baird. Maggie studied theatre and dance at university and plays the piano and guitar.

* Maggie married fellow actor Patrick O'Connell in 1995. They met while performing in the same show in Alaska.

* Maggie was a member of the Los Angeles comedy group The Groundlings in the 1990s, alongside stars like Will Ferrell and Kristen Wiig.

* Maggie also taught improv comedy to Melissa McCarthy, future star of movies like *Bridesmaids*, *Spy*, and *Ghostbusters*.

* As an actor, Billie's mother has appeared on hit shows, like *The X-Files*, *Bones* and *Six Feet Under*.

* She's also a voice actor and can be heard in video games, such as *Saints Row*, *Final Fantasy* and the *Mass Effect* series, where she played a psychic alien called Samara.

MOM & DAD!

* In 2009 Maggie released an album of country music called *We Sail*.

* In 2013 Maggie wrote, produced and starred in a movie called *Life Inside Out*. She even recorded the soundtrack herself.

* Billie's dad, Patrick O'Connell, is also an actor and musician. He can play lots of instruments, including the ukulele!

* Patrick can be seen playing a reporter in the first *Iron Man* movie and also played an army general on the *Supergirl* TV show!

* Like Maggie, Patrick also does voice-over work for video games. In 2016 he voiced an evil Swedish businessman in the game *Hitman*, who players could kill by dropping a giant moose statue on his head!

OH, BROTHER!

HE'S THE CO-WRITER AND PRODUCER BEHIND ALL OF BILLIE'S SONGS AND ALSO HER BIG BROTHER! MEET FINNEAS O'CONNELL...

Finneas was born on 30th July, 1997. That's four years before Billie came along!

If you want to know why Billie has 'Pirate' as one of her middle names, ask Finneas! It was his idea!

Billie's breakout hit, *ocean eyes*, was originally supposed to be a song for The Slightlys, but Finneas gave it to his sister instead. Aw!

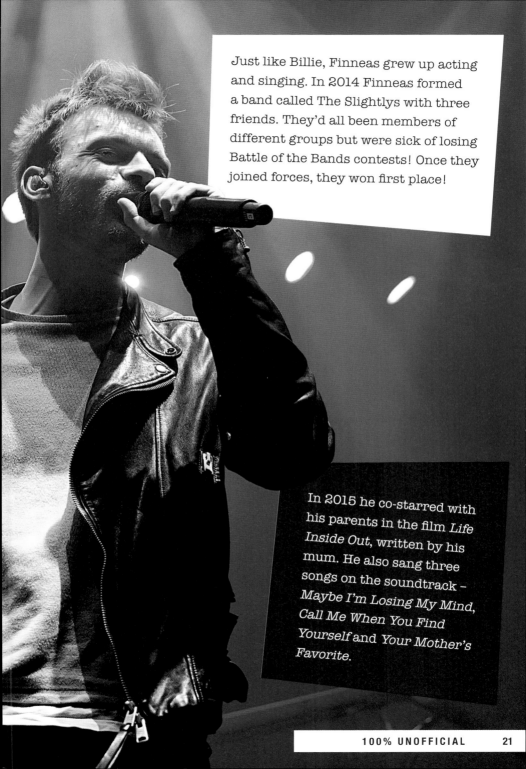

Just like Billie, Finneas grew up acting and singing. In 2014 Finneas formed a band called The Slightlys with three friends. They'd all been members of different groups but were sick of losing Battle of the Bands contests! Once they joined forces, they won first place!

In 2015 he co-starred with his parents in the film *Life Inside Out*, written by his mum. He also sang three songs on the soundtrack – *Maybe I'm Losing My Mind*, *Call Me When You Find Yourself* and *Your Mother's Favorite*.

SOLO CAREER

FINNEAS ALSO RECORDS HIS OWN SOLO SONGS. HIS FIRST SOLO SINGLE, *NEW GIRL*, CAME OUT IN 2016.

As well as working with Billie on her material, Finneas has somehow found time to release another NINE solo singles of his own! Does he never sleep?

As an actor, Finneas made his movie debut as one of the students in the Cameron Diaz comedy *Bad Teacher*.

Finneas's most famous acting role was as Alistair in the final season of *Glee*. He appeared in four episodes, took part in several big musical numbers and even made out with Spencer!

You can also see Finneas as Ronnie Jr in the TV sitcom *Modern Family,* and he appeared in the scary serial killer drama *Aquarius.*

ANIMAL MAGIC

PEPPER

BILLIE HAS ALWAYS LOVED ANIMALS; SHE EVEN INCLUDES SOME IN HER MUSIC VIDEOS.

Pepper is Billie's beloved dog — she's a pit bull mix. Pepper has been a member of the family since Billie was little, and Billie fell in love with her when she first saw her at the rescue shelter. Almost all of Billie's pets are rescue animals.

FOSTER PUPPIES

Billie took it upon herself to share some love by fostering two pit bull puppies from Angel City Pit Bulls – a non-profit rescue organisation based in Los Angeles, California – during the stressful struggles of social isolation.

Billie posted some adorable pictures of the puppies on her Insta stories, alongside the caption, 'If you're looking for things to do while we're all stuck at home, foster some babiieesss.'

COOLI THE TARANTULA

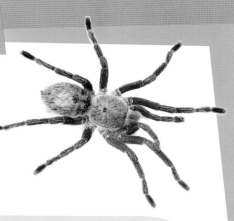

If you look at the creepy critters crawling all over her face during the video for 'you should see me in a crown', you'll know that not only is Billie not scared of spiders, she absolutely loves them! Billie even had a pet tarantula called Cooli.

'You should come over and see him,' she told a fan during an on-stage interview at the Grammy Museum. 'He's blue, and he's very cute. They're fun. They're not gonna hurt you. They're cool. They have personalities.'

James Corden was less impressed when he met Cooli while filming Carpool Karaoke with Billie. He reluctantly let the spider walk on his hand – and then Billie left the room, trapping him with the spider! Sadly, Cooli died in December 2019, having lived much longer than most pet spiders. RIP, little dude!

MISHA THE CAT

Billie's family has also had several cats. The most recent addition to the family was Misha. Like most of their other pets, she was rehomed from a shelter.

TOURETTE'S SYNDROME?

IN NOVEMBER 2018 A VIDEO CIRCULATED ONLINE SHOWING A COMPILATION OF CLIPS FROM INTERVIEWS IN WHICH BILLIE WOULD TWITCH HER HEAD UNEXPECTEDLY OR BULGE AND BLINK HER EYES. BILLIE RESPONDED IN AN INSTAGRAM POST AND REVEALED THAT SHE HAS SOMETHING CALLED TOURETTE'S SYNDROME.

Tourette's syndrome is a brain condition, which causes people to make involuntary sounds and movements known as 'tics'. In rare cases, people with Tourette's also shout out rude words or random phrases. These sudden outbursts are hard – sometimes impossible – to control.

About one in every hundred people have Tourette's syndrome. That means worldwide there are over seven million people with the condition.

In an interview with *The Fader* magazine, Billie explained more. 'It's confusing when someone is making a weird face gesture or throwing out their neck. The internet hasn't really seen the bad ones because I'm really good at suppressing them.

The thing is, the longer you suppress them, the worse they get afterwards.'

'I'm sure one day everyone will see the tic attacks that happen when I'm stressed and haven't slept. But it could be a lot worse and it's not, and I'm grateful for that.'

SEEING SOUND!

BOTH BILLIE AND HER BROTHER FINNEAS HAVE SOMETHING CALLED SYNAESTHESIA. THIS IS AN UNUSUAL PHENOMENON WHERE PEOPLE'S SENSES ARE CONNECTED IN UNUSUAL WAYS, SO HEARING BELLS RINGING MIGHT MAKE THEM SEE THE COLOUR YELLOW, OR THE WORD 'TUESDAY' MIGHT TASTE OF STRAWBERRIES.

It's especially useful for creative people, such as Bllie and Finneas, because it allows them to think of music as more than just something to listen to and helps them come up with ideas for videos that reflect the feelings of each song.

'Everything that I make I'm already thinking of what colour it is, and what texture it is, and what day of the week it is, and what number it is and what shape,' Billie told *iHeartRadio*. 'We both have it so we think about everything this way.'

Billie thinks of Finneas as an orange triangle, but when she thinks about his name it's dark green!

Synaesthesia is quite common among artists and musicians. The famous painter Vincent Van Gogh was believed to have it, as do modern pop stars such as Pharrell Williams, Charli XCX and Lorde.

' I want to give people the smallest amount of what it's like in my brain. '

Billie describes her song *Bury a Friend* as 'grey, black, brown, anything dark', while the song *Xanny* feels like velvet, 'like if you could feel smoke'.

Bad guy is 'yellow but also red and the number seven. It's not hot but warm, like an oven. And it smells like cookies.'

BILLIE  DANCING

IN A 2017 INTERVIEW, BILLIE SAID, 'I THINK IF A SONG DOESN'T MAKE YOU OR YOU CAN'T DANCE TO IT, THEN IT'S NOT A SONG'. NO SURPRISE, COMING FROM SOMEONE WHOSE FIRST LOVE WAS ALWAYS DANCING.

'Dance has been in my life since I was really little,' Billie says. 'I always dance when performing live, and I make it a point to incorporate it into my videos. I think it's cool that dance isn't a forgotten or lost dream of mine because, as an artist and singer, I get to dance. I also find that movement is a great outlet for me to feel, however it is I'm feeling inside, and give the most honest performance of song.'

PHOTO

t, she wasn't busting the kind of shaky, spooky moves
er videos today. She was more inspired by Shirley Temple,
ie star from the 1930s famous for her tap dancing. Billie
pped an interest in hip hop dancing, though, and set her
career as a dancer. An injury put an end to that but meant
usic took off instead, so it all worked out pretty well!

DANCE LIKE BILLIE

quat or crawl for quieter moments.
eeping arm movements when the music gets louder.
shoulder then the other in time to the beat.
y with your body — all of Billie's dance routines are
nnected to her emotions and lyrics.

KEEPING BUSY

THOUGH SHE SPENDS MOST OF HER TIME WRITING AND RECORDING NEW SONGS, BILLIE HAS HAD LOTS OF DIFFERENT HOBBIES AND JOBS.

Billie designs her own clothes, as well as customising things she already owns to suit her style. She's particularly fond of wearing them back to front or turning old clothes inside out to show off the seams.

Billie loves hanging out with her friends but finds it frustrating when she has to leave them to go on tour. By the time she comes back, she's missed out on months of gossip and everyone has new in-jokes, which she doesn't get.

She had more fun recording background dialogue for movies such as *Diary of a Wimpy Kid* and *X-Men Apocalypse*. She describes the work as 'a bunch of kids in a room yelling random things, and then we'd have a break and get snacks'. Sounds like a sweet deal!

When she was little, Billie would use her dad's camera to shoot funny photo

stories using her toy animals. Her dad would then turn them into videos,

which he still keeps in a folder on his computer called 'Billie's World'.

Billie constantly doodles and writes, and she carries a notebook with her everywhere, which she fills with drawings of things she's dreamed about or scribbles down ideas for new songs and videos.

Billie has always been a fan of horses and often makes time when she's touring to find a way to go for a ride. When she was younger, she even volunteered at a horse stable close to her house, cleaning out the stables in exchange for riding lessons.

TRUE OR FALSE?

1. Billie's middle name is Pirate because she looked like Captain Jack Sparrow as a baby.

2. When she was four years old, Billie wrote a song about falling into a black hole.

3. Billie's brother is called Ferb.

4. Billie's mum played an alien in a *Mass Effect* video game.

5. Billie's dad is in the *Iron Man* movie.

6. Billie almost played the character Rue in *The Hunger Games*.

7. Billie's song *Fingers Crossed* was inspired by *The Walking Dead* TV show.

8. Finneas wrote *ocean eyes* for his band, The Slightlys.

9. The only time that Billie has eaten meat in her life was when she swallowed an ant by mistake.

10. Billie can play the bagpipes.

11. Billie used to post on Instagram under the username @riderofthewind.

12. Billie is allergic to avocados and throws up if she touches them.

13. Billie once wrote a song about Justin Bieber as a baby called 'Baby Boo Boo Bieber'.

14. Billie is the cousin of popular *Fortnite* player Ninja.

15. The song *bellyache* is about a murderer.

16. Billie's synaesthesia means she thinks of her brother as an orange triangle.

17. Billie had never heard of James Bond before being asked to record the theme to *No Time To Die*.

18. Billie is not allowed to have fizzy drinks.

19. Billie loves spiders and had a pet tarantula.

20. Billie has her own brand of vegan cheese called It's D-eilish-us.

21. Billie holds the world record for being the youngest female artist to have a UK number one album.

22. Billie deliberately wears baggy, over-sized clothes so people can't make comments about her body.

23. Billie is afraid of the dark.

24. Billie taught former president Barack Obama how to dab.

25. Billie speaks fluent Spanish and Japanese.

26. Billie's natural hair colour is ginger.

27. Billie's favourite TV show is *The Office*.

28. The name Eilish means "hushed voice" in Gaelic.

BILLIE IS FAMOUS FOR HER LOVE OF BAGGY, SHAPELESS CLOTHING. FOR HER, IT'S A WAY OF PROTECTING HERSELF FROM THE SORT OF CONSTANT DEGRADING ATTENTION THAT OTHER FEMALE CELEBRITIES GET FROM THE MEDIA.

'If I was a guy and I was wearing these baggy clothes, nobody would bat an eye,' she says.

'There's people out there saying, "Dress like a girl for once! Wear tight clothes, you'd be much prettier, and your career would be so much better! No, it wouldn't. It literally would not.

One thing Billie is particularly great at is colour coordination. She'll pick a bright accent colour, usually for her top, and then echo that colour choice throughout the outfit.

With that in mind, here are some of Billie's most amazing outfits – and some ideas of how you can rock her style with confidence too!

THINK COLOURFUL

This kicking yellow T-shirt would look great by itself, but check out the yellow necklace and laces and the darker yellow patches on those NEW FTR LDN joggers. It all ties together and looks amazing!

CRAZY CARTOONS

Billie often wears clothing with big, bold cartoon characters, such as this shirt and shorts set that she chose to perform in at Glastonbury. The characters are Blue Meanies from The Beatles' movie *Yellow Submarine*, and the clothes were designed by Stella McCartney whose dad, Paul, was in The Beatles.

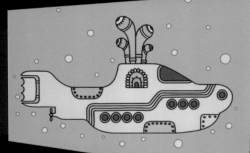

Billie grew up listening to The Beatles with her dad, so this is an outfit that doesn't just look cool, it has personal meaning for her too.

BE UNIQUE

Even a dark outfit can pop with the right style, and Billie isn't afraid to seek out unique designers rather than relying on the same big names as other stars. This funky outfit features characters from the 1990s anime series *Sailor Moon* and was hand-painted by a New York artist called SlumpyKev! For a typical Billie finishing touch, she accessorised with some simple chains and oversized A$AP Rocky Under Armor sneakers.

MAKE IT YOUR OWN

THE ACADEMY AWARDS IS ONE OF THE GLITZIEST AND MOST PRESTIGIOUS EVENTS ON THE CELEBRITY CALENDAR, WITH STARS SHOWING OFF THEIR SLINKIEST DESIGNER DRESSES AND TUXEDOS.

How did Billie turn up? Well, she went with a designer – Chanel – but everything else about this boxy woollen suit is pure Eilish!

Those extra-long nails, matching black buttons and black hair are the perfect contrast. And, of course, she didn't wear posh high heels — she went with a trusty pair of trainers!

BE BOLD

The best fashion also makes an artistic statement, and that's definitely true of this colourfully weird outfit that Billie wore to a special Spotify promotional event in Los Angeles. This head-to-toe ensemble was designed by Louis Vuitton. The brightly coloured symbols and the dribbly paint patterns are eye-catching enough, but it's the superhero-style mask and large summer hat that make it unmistakably Billie – even if you can't see her face!

WORD UP!

ANOTHER CLASSIC EXAMPLE OF BILLIE'S STYLE IS WEARING CLOTHES THAT HAVE SLOGANS OR WORDS IN STRANGE, OR EVEN UGLY LAYOUTS. THINK OF IT AS A DELIBERATE ACT OF ANTI-FASHION!

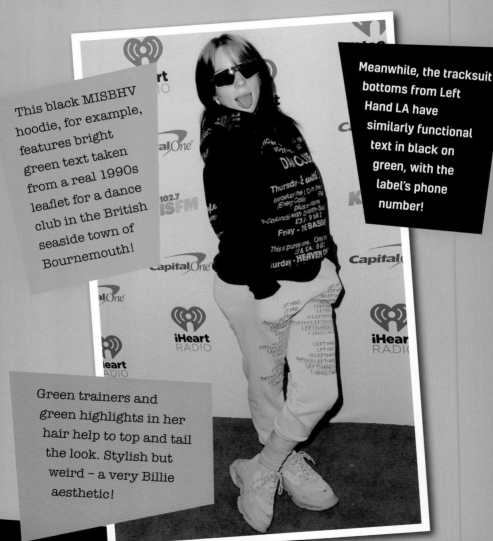

This black MISBHV hoodie, for example, features bright green text taken from a real 1990s leaflet for a dance club in the British seaside town of Bournemouth!

Meanwhile, the tracksuit bottoms from Left Hand LA have similarly functional text in black on green, with the label's phone number!

Green trainers and green highlights in her hair help to top and tail the look. Stylish but weird – a very Billie aesthetic!

DESIGN IT YOURSELF

Although she often dresses in designer clothes for fancy events, Billie has created her own affordable clothing line for high street chain H&M. With loose fits and lots of cream and black spikes with bright colours, it's unmistakably Billie's style.

Best of all, every design is sustainable and environmentally friendly, using recycled materials. Looking good and saving the planet? That's so Billie.

BILLIE'S
FAVOURITE THINGS!

BILLIE IS NEVER SHY ABOUT THE STUFF SHE LOVES. SHE'LL NAMECHECK IT IN INTERVIEWS, TALK ABOUT IT ON SOCIAL MEDIA, EVEN WRITE SONGS ABOUT IT! THESE ARE JUST SOME OF THE THINGS SHE'S SHOUTED ABOUT IN THE PAST.

THE BABADOOK

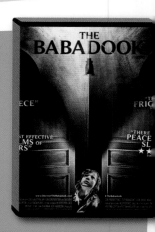

Billie absolutely adores horror movies, and one of her all-time favourites is *The Babadook*, the chilling 2014 movie about a single mother and her weird son who are plagued a mysterious monster from a storybook.

'One of my favourite movies in the world,' Billie explained when a fan asked her on Instagram what inspired the cover to her first album.

'*The Babadook* was the complete main inspiration for [the album].' Creepy!

THE WALKING DEAD

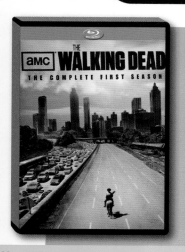

As a horror nut, it's no surprise that Billie loves the gory zombie TV show *The Walking Dead*. It was even the inspiration for one of her earliest songs, 'fingers crossed'. Talking about the lyrics in an interview with *Harper's Bazaar* magazine, she explained: 'I literally just watched *The Walking Dead* and I took little lines from it. Just watch all of *The Walking Dead*, and you'll find some things that are in my song and some episode titles that are in my song'.

THE OFFICE

Although Billie has a soft spot in her heart for horror, she also loves a good comedy. One of her faves is the American version of TV sitcom *The Office*. She loved it so much that she sampled dialogue from the 2011 episode 'Threat Level Midnight' for 'my strange addiction'. 'We literally just ripped the audio from Netflix and put it in the song,' she told *MTV News*. The creators and cast of the show were thrilled, and actor Rainn Wilson who played Dwight Schrute on the show – even surprised her at home to quiz her on *The Office* trivia! Needless to say, she crushed it!

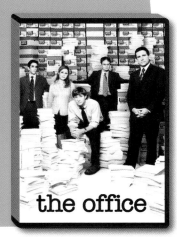

the office

VEGAN BURRITOS

Billie loves spicy food and avocados, and especially vegan burritos. She absolutely adores them! Billie posted an Instagram video in July 2019 of her ordering Taco Bell drive-thru, saying, 'I'm going to get 18 bean burritos with only beans, nothing else, only beans inside. Only beans. Eighteen burritos, and only beans. You know what? Make that 20'. Hope she opened the window after eating all of that!

SPIRITED AWAY

Seeing this 2001 Japanese animated fantasy as kids was a huge influence on both Billie and Finneas. The eerie character 'No Face' was a particular favourite thanks to his spooky gliding motion.

'When Finneas saw *Spirited Away*, he was so scared of the parents turning into pigs that he had to go to therapy for years!' Billie said in an interview with Noisey.

'I was like, yeah! I would watch it over and over. I thought it was so dope!'

BILLIE'S FAVE FOOD!

BILLIE'S GO-TO COMFORT FOOD DISH IS A VEGAN BURRITO, WITH PLENTY OF AVOCADO. HERE'S HOW TO MAKE ONE, JUST IN CASE SHE POPS IN FOR LUNCH. HEY, IT COULD HAPPEN!

Burritos are super flexible – you can swap any of the herbs, spices and veggies to suit your taste.

Ingredients

1 large tortilla
a splash of olive oil
1 clove of garlic, crushed
1 tin of black beans
1 teaspoon of cumin
1 teaspoon of oregano
1 pinch each of salt and pepper
1/2 teaspoon of chilli flakes
250 g rice
vegan sour cream to taste
1 handful of chopped lettuce
1 tomato, finely chopped
1 avocado, thinly sliced
1 small tin of sweetcorn
1 red pepper, finely chopped
vegan cheese, grated to taste
1 tablespoon of freshly chopped coriander

Instructions

Always ask an adult to help with knives and hot ovens if you need them!

1. Warm the oven to 180C or Gas Mark 4, and place the tortilla in for a few minutes to warm up.
2. Boil the rice until soft and set aside.
3. Heat the oil in a large frying pan over a medium heat, and cook the garlic for a minute or so until soft.
4. Drain and add the beans, followed by the cumin, oregano, salt, pepper and chilli flakes. Fry until the beans are warmed through.
5. Place your warm tortilla on a large flat surface. Add the sour cream, lettuce, tomato, avocado, sweetcorn and red pepper in a tidy pile in the centre of the tortilla. Leave a little more room at the top of the tortilla than at the bottom to help with rolling it up later.
6. Now add the beans, rice, grated cheese and coriander. Try and keep the pile neat and tidy. You can press the ingredients into a small plastic tub and tip them onto the tortilla to help them keep their shape.
7. Time to roll! With the tortilla in front of you, roll the left and right sides in first, and then fold up the bottom edge of the tortilla. Now carefully keep rolling up towards the top edge until you have a nice, neat burrito parcel!
8. Wrap the burrito tightly in foil. You can freeze it for later, warm it in the oven or just cut it in half and eat right now!

HOW WELL DO YOU KNOW BILLIE?

HOW MUCH DO YOU KNOW ABOUT BILLIE'S LIFE, CAREER AND MUSIC? FIND OUT IF YOU'RE A BILLIE SUPER-FAN WITH THIS QUIZ! THE ANSWERS ARE ON PAGE 90.

1. What is the name of the Los Angeles' neighbourhood where Billie lives and grew up?

2. What is Billie's star sign?

3. Which Marvel movie does Billie's dad have a small role in?

4. Billie wrote a song at the age of four about falling into what?

5. What year was Finneas born?

6. Billie once wrote a song inspired by *The Walking Dead*. What was it called?

7. What was Billie's favourite animal as a child?

8. 'Ocean eyes' was written for Finneas' band. What are they called?

9. Why did Billie record 'ocean eyes'?

10. Which music website was 'ocean eyes' uploaded to?

11. Billie is vegan, but how did she once accidentally eat meat?

12. Who did Billie collaborate with on the song 'lovely'?

13. What is Billie's fruit-related Instagram account username?

14. What was Finneas' character called on *Glee*?

15. What is the unusual title of the first track on *WHEN WE FALL ASLEEP, WHERE DO WE GO?*

16. The song *you should see me in a crown* takes its name from a quote on which TV show?

17. After a video of her circulated online, Billie revealed she has which neurological condition?

18. Which of Billie's songs appeared on the soundtrack for the first season of *13 Reasons Why*?

19. At the 2020 Academy Awards, Billie performed which song by a classic 1960s pop group?

20. What was the name of Billie's first ever live tour in 2017?

21. Which was Billie's first single to reach number one in the United States?

22. And which of her songs was the first to reach number one in the UK?

23. Where is Billie's favourite place to write songs?

24. What is on Billie's face in the video for 'you should see me in a crown'?

25. Which of Billie's songs was inspired by a video game?

26. Before she was famous, Billie recorded background voices for which superhero movie?

27. Both Billie and Finneas have an unusual ability that mixes up their senses and lets them 'see' sounds. What is it called?

28. Billie broke a world record by having how many singles on the US Billboard Hot 100 chart at the same time?

29. One of Billie's middle names is Pirate. Who gave her that name?

30. Which of Billie's musical heroes made a guest appearance on a special version of *bad guy*?

SCRAPBOOK

BILLIE HAS GIVEN SOME AMAZING AND INVENTIVE LIV[E]
PERFORMANCES ALL OVER THE WORLD, SO HERE'S A
PHOTO ALBUM OF HER BEST STAGE MOMENTS!

SWISS MUSIC AWARDS

Lucerne, Switzerland, February 2019

Billie turned down the colour for a soulful acoustic set at this prestigious European awards show. She was back at the same event in 2020 where she picked up the awards for Best Breaking Act International and Best Solo Act International!

TIVOLIVREDENBURG

Utrecht, Netherlands, February 2019
Billie gave a particularly energetic show at this famous concert hall in the Netherlands, with a stage set that was designed to look like a giant spider made of lights!

GLASTONBURY FESTIVAL

Somerset, UK, July 2019
Billie rocked the Other Stage at the world-famous Glastonbury Festival, where over 200,000 people flocked to Worthy Farm for a week of live music from stars such as Stormzy, Miley Cyrus and, of course, Billie! Music mag *NME* called her performance a 'once-in-a-generation show'.

LOLLAPALOOZA FESTIVAL

Berlin, Germany, September 2019
Thousands of Billie's German fans packed Berlin's Olympic Stadium for this two-day festival. Also on the bill were rockers Rage Against The Machine, rap duo Run The Jewels and DJ blackbear, who remixed *ocean eyes* for Billie back in 2016.

ACADEMY AWARDS

Los Angeles, USA, February 2020

Dressed all in black, Billie performed a beautiful cover version of The Beatles' *Yesterday* during the biggest movie awards on the planet. The song accompanied the show's In Memoriam section, which honoured all the actors and other film industry people who had died during the year.

PALAU SANT JORDI

Barcelona, Spain, September 2019

The Palau Sant Jordi is Spain's biggest indoor venue and holds over 17,000 people. Looking at the size of this crowd, it's hard to believe that only a few years earlier Billie had never performed professionally and was playing to tiny crowds in clubs!

WE KNOW THAT *OCEAN EYES* WAS ORIGINALLY WRITTEN BY FINNEAS FOR HIS BAND, THE SLIGHTLYS, BUT WHAT IS THE SONG ABOUT?

The lyrics are written from the perspective of someone talking about a former lover and how they make them feel. The image of falling into the ocean is repeated throughout the song, just how the singer would fall into their lover's eyes and get lost.

The first verse contrasts the water imagery with references to 'burning cities' and 'napalm skies'. Napalm was a chemical weapon used during the Vietnam War designed to set fire to jungles. The lover is made to sound exciting but also dangerous and destructive.

In the second verse, the phrase 'diamond mind' is used twice. The first time, it seems to refer to the lover's mind as something exotic and beautiful. The second time, the singer refers to their own mind, now made hard and unbreakable like a diamond.

Can you hear the weird backwards singing near the end of the song? That's the chorus, sung back to front with the last line first, and then reversed.

Billie was sending her friend a Snapchat and put the reverse filter on while we were working on the song and it sounded sick,' Finneas explained in a later interview.

'So I took every vocal from the chorus and reversed them and washed them out with reverb to create the bridge. Crashed my computer.'

> ❛ The image of falling into the ocean is repeated throughout the song. ❜

#KR

US music site *Stereogum* called the song 'pure pop', *Vogue* magazine said it was 'profound' and *Billboard* – the official magazine of the US charts – said it was 'understated and heartbreaking'. Not bad for a song recorded in a bedroom for a dance class!

BILLIE'S SONGS DECODED

BILLIE AND FINNEAS SPEND A LOT OF TIME ON LYRICS, AND EACH SONG HAS A PARTICULAR STORY OR MEANING. IF YOU WERE WONDERING WHAT SOME OF HER MOST POPULAR SONGS ARE ABOUT, READ ON TO DISCOVER THE TRUTH!

BELLYACHE

Billie has said that this song is about guilt – in particular the guilt she felt as a little kid when she would steal something or take toys away from friends. 'I used to think the police were going to come to class and take me away from my parents,' she told *NME* magazine. Billie took this real memory and emotion and worked it into a fictional song about a killer with bipolar disorder.

BAD GUY

This song is about the fake personalities that people put on in order to impress others, particularly people who claim to be wild, bad and dangerous. 'If you're going around all the time saying like, "Yeah, I'm bad, I'm always breaking rules, and doing this and doing that." You're not,' Billie told NME. She also likes the idea of a girl using the phrase 'bad guy' to describe herself, because it catches people off guard.

XANNY

This song is about kids being pressured to try drugs. 'I don't want my friends to die anymore,' she told *The Guardian* newspaper. She came up with the idea for the song while bored at a party where everyone else was getting drunk and behaving like different people. 'I have never done drugs,' she explained. 'I've never got high, I've never smoked anything in my life. It's just not interesting to me.'

WHEN THE PARTY'S OVER

This song is a kind of sequel to 'party favor', and both are about breaking up with a toxic boyfriend. 'It's like, you're on the phone with someone and you can't hear them, they can't hear you, it's loud, they're mad at you for some reason. I feel like everybody's had that struggle with someone – somebody on the phone yelling for some reason,' Billie told New Zealand magazine *Coup de Main*.

> ❛ I've never got high, I've never smoked anything in my life. It's just not interesting to me. ❜

YOU SHOULD SEE ME IN A CROWN

This song was inspired by a quote from the villainous Moriarty in the BBC show *Sherlock* and is written from the perspective of somebody dangerous preparing to show the world what they're capable of. 'I feel like if I heard that, I'd be freaked out and I love being freaked out, so I really want to freak other people out,' Billie told *Billboard* magazine.

COPYCAT

This one is pretty easy to work out just from the title! It's about a girl who copied everything Billie did to be like her. 'I'm like, can you not?' Billie told music website *Genius*. 'I already exist! Why would you want to… it's so weird!' Lines such as 'dirty water, poison rain' show two things that are kind of the same, but only one sounds cool and interesting. You can guess which one is Billie!

EVERYTHING I WANTED

...s of Billie's songs reference sleep and dreams, and 'everything i wan...
...s inspired by a nightmare she had where she jumped off the Golden...
...te Bridge in San Francisco and nobody cared. 'All of my best friends...
...ople that I worked with basically came out in public and said, like, "...
...e never liked her,"' she told Radio 1 DJ Annie Mac. 'In the dream, th...
...dn't care... it really did mess me up.'

WISH YOU WERE GAY

This is another song based directly on one of Billie's own experi...
boy she was in love with rejected her, so she wrote this song a...
reaction. 'The whole idea of the song is... you don't love me be...
don't love me and that's the only reason, and I wish you didn't...
because you didn't love girls," she said in an interview with Pd...
revealed on Instagram that boy did later admit to her that he...

ILOMILO

You might think this tender song, full of regret and longing, is about a failed relationship, but it's actually about something much simpler: an Xbox video game! 'I loved ilomilo'; that was like my favourite game in the world,' Billie said on the *Hot Ones* YouTube show. 'The whole idea of the game is just losing the person you love and then finding them again.'

LOVELY [WITH KHALID]

Billie's collaboration with Khalid is about a couple struggling to stay together through a period of dark depression. In the video, Billie and Khalid are trapped in a glass box which fills with freezing water until they both disappear. The title, as Billie explained to DJ Zane Lowe, is meant to be ironic. 'The song was really freaking depressing so then it's like oh, how lovely. Just taking everything horrible, like, you know what? This is great. I'm so happy being miserable.'

IDONTWANNABEYOUANYMORE

Thanks to her bold and brash style, it's easy to think of Billie as confident and comfortable in her own skin. This song shows the other side to her, as she wrestles with feelings of inadequacy and self-loathing. Billie has described it as the opposite to *COPYCAT*. 'You wanna be me? I look at the mirror over here, and I don't wanna be you,' she explained to *Genius*. 'It's so annoying to feel like this all the time.'

BURY A FRIEND

Billie says that this is the song that helped her define the sound and style for her album. It's a dark obsessive song that Billie says is written from the perspective of the monster under your bed. But don't take that literally! 'Anything could be the monster,' she told *Rolling Stone* magazine. 'It could be someone you love so much that it's taking over your life. I think love and terror and hatred are all the same thing.'

BILLIE'S SONGS CONTAIN SOME AMAZING AND
BEAUTIFUL LYRICS, BUT HOW WELL DO YOU KNOW
HER WORK? IDENTIFY WHICH SONGS THESE LINES
COME FROM. THE ANSWERS ARE ON PAGE 90.

1. 'If you don't stop, I'll call your dad...'

2. 'My Lucifer is lonely...'

3. 'I guess being lonely fits me...'

4. 'Heart made of glass, my mind of stone...'

5. 'I'm home alone, you're God knows where...'

6. 'Tore my shirt to stop you bleeding...'

7. 'Bite my glass, set myself on fire...'

8. 'We knew right from the start that you'd fall apart...'

9. 'When the world is silent and the days are long...'

10. 'It feels like yesterday was a year ago...'

11. 'That's what a year-long headache does to you...'

12. 'Can you check your Uber rating?'

13. 'I wanna make 'em scared...'

14. 'By the way, you've been uninvited...'

15. 'He ain't a man and sure as hell ain't honest...'

16. 'Careful creature made friends with time...'

17. 'If I could get to sleep, I would have slept by now...'

18. 'The blood you bleed is just the blood you owe...'

19. 'My mommy likes to sing along...'

20. 'I'm gonna run this nothing town...'

BILLIE'S INFLUENCES

BILLIE NOW INSPIRES THOUSANDS OF FANS WITH HER MUSIC, BUT WHO ARE THE ACTS THAT SHE LOOKS UP TO FOR INSPIRATION? HERE ARE SOME OF THE ARTISTS SHE'S BIGGED UP IN INTERVIEWS...

AVRIL LAVIGNE

Billie is a big fan of the *Sk8er Boi* singer, which is just as well because she's often compared to the 'Pop Punk Queen'. When they finally met, Billie posted a selfie of them both with the caption 'THANK YOU FOR MAKING ME WHAT I AM'. Of course, Lavigne had her first hit song at the age of 15 and was signed to a major recording deal because of a tape she made at home. Hmm, sounds familiar!

Billie often credits this rapper as her number one inspiration, both in music and in style. Originally part of the hip hop group Odd Future, Tyler went solo in 2009 and has since become one the biggest names in independent music. His lyrics have been controversial, but he's carved his own unique path to fame – something Billie definitely identifies with!

TYLER, THE CREATOR

LANA DEL REY

Billie's hushed vocal style was influenced by Lana Del Rey, but Billie is uncomfortable with people comparing them. When she was introduced to Del Rey at an awards event, the singer patted Billie on the head! 'I wouldn't let anyone else pat me on the head,' Billie said later, 'but it was her, so I was cool.'

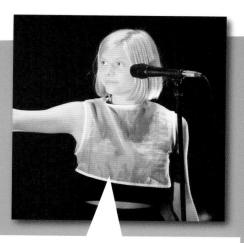

You may not have heard of this Norwegian pop star, but it was only after stumbling across the video for Aurora's song *Runaway* on YouTube that Billie decided to pursue a career in music.

AURORA

SPICE GIRLS

Billie loved the Spice Girls' music as a kid but didn't realise they were a real group. She thought they were invented for the movie *Spice World* and were played by actors!

Billie grew up listening to The Beatles, probably the biggest pop band in history, because her dad would put their songs on mixtapes for her. It paid off! Billie and Finneas performed their song *Yesterday* at the Academy Awards.

THE BEATLES

MAKING MUSIC

Billie likes to write in a treehouse that her dad built in their back garden. She climbs up with her ukulele and a notebook and sits there to play and write. She's been doing this since she was a little girl and especially likes it when the weather is windy or rainy. 'I still go up there all the time,' she says.

It's often said that Billie's first album was recorded in Finneas's bedroom, and that's not an urban myth! It's not even an empty bedroom that was turned into a studio, it was his actual bedroom! He would sit at his computer while Billie sat on his bed to record her vocals.

EVERYONE KNOWS THAT BILLIE AND FINNEAS WRITE AND RECORD ALL OF BILLIE'S MUSIC TOGETHER, BUT HOW DOES THAT WORK? LUCKILY FOR CURIOUS FANS, THE PAIR HAVE NEVER BEEN SECRETIVE ABOUT THEIR WORKING METHODS.

Finneas prefers to compose music using an old upright piano that used to belong to their grandfather. Once he's got a tune he likes, he uses a digital keyboard connected to his computer to record it so that he can tweak the sound until it suits the song. Usually he starts with an idea for the song title, and then works out what the song should be from that.

Even though Finneas has now moved into his own house, only a few minutes away, he still likes to have recording equipment set up in his room.

'I just have a lot of fun in there creating ideas. The best part about having everything in my room is that as soon as I've written something I'm excited about I can just turn my microphone on and record it,' he says.

Finneas believes that recording the album in a normal bedroom helped to give the music a unique feel. 'The bedroom has a very specific sound, very tight and intimate and closed and quiet,' he says. 'I love the way it makes vocals sound.'

WORKING TOGETHER

BILLIE PREFERS WORKING WITH FINNEAS BECAUSE SHE THINKS PEOPLE WASTE TOO MUCH TIME WHEN WRITING WITH STRANGERS, TRYING TO BE POLITE ABOUT EACH OTHER'S IDEAS. SHE SAYS 'WITH FINNEAS IT'S JUST LIKE, "NO, THAT SUCKS, LET'S MOVE ON." WE JUST KNOW EACH OTHER SO WE CAN DO THAT.'

When they record Billie's second album, it will probably be in Finneas's new house – but they might go back to the old bedroom for some songs.

'Maybe sometimes there will be just a vocal that we feel we must record in that room just to make it sound that way,' says Finneas.

Finneas loves to record unusual sounds and then use those to create virtual instruments for recording. Among the noises he used to make Billie's album are a stick falling out of a tree, a dentist's drill, a toy oven and their dad sharpening a kitchen knife!

Their lyrics are sometimes based on things that either Billie or Finneas have experienced or felt, but they also love to write songs that are nothing to do with their real lives.

'We like to completely make up things and become characters,' explains Billie.

'We like to have songs that are really fictional.'

Billie and Finneas love being able to just make music without having to get anyone else involved.

'When I was starting to make music, I thought I had to pay a bunch of people to do all my things professionally and that that would be the only way I would ever have any success,' says Finneas.

'It's really important for kids to not think that there's something intangible and out of reach for them. The truth is that you just have to make a song that people like.'

BE LIKE BILLIE!

YOU MAY LOOK AT BILLIE, RECORDING HER ALBUM FROM A BEDROOM AT HOME, AND WONDER 'CAN I DO THAT TOO?' AND THE ANSWER IS YES! OF COURSE YOU CAN! IT'S EASIER THAN EVER TO MAKE PROFESSIONAL-SOUNDING MUSIC, AND IT'S NOT AS EXPENSIVE AS YOU THINK. HERE'S WHAT YOU'LL NEED...

Computer
Obviously! Any kind of computer will do — it doesn't have to be super fancy. Most professionals use MacBooks for audio recording, but PCs are good too.

Audio Interface
This gadget plugs into your computer and carries the signal from whatever instrument or microphone you plug into the other side to your computer. This is the one thing you'll probably need to spend a little extra on, but it's the difference between getting flat, tinny-sounding audio and pro-level sound that you can really work with. Search online for 'AudioBox' or 'AVID Pro Tools Duet'.

Microphone
You can pick up really cheap microphones online, but they'll give you poor sound quality for music. Professional studios use lots of different mics for different instruments, but for recording your singing you should search for a 'large diaphragm condenser vocal mic'. You'll also want a stand to keep the mic steady.

Headphones

You'll need a good set of headphones. Your tangled earbuds won't do the job! The cost can vary a lot, but just make sure you buy 'open back' headphones — these will isolate only the sounds you need to hear when mixing.

DAW

DAW, or Digital Audio Workstation, is the software that lets you take your recordings and really play around with them. Most importantly, it lets you edit different tracks, so you can separate out guitars, bass, drums, vocals, move them around, add effects and build the perfect pop song. The good news is that you can try a very popular professional DAW for free — just search for 'AVID Pro Tools First'.

Speakers

A decent pair of speakers lets you play your tunes back to see how they sound. Watch out for high street models as they are often designed to boost different parts of the music. That's not what you want — you need to hear what the music sounds like 'raw'. Search for 'studio monitors' instead.

Instruments

Here's the tricky part. If you have your own instruments already, perfect! But if you're starting from scratch then a decent MIDI keyboard will let you recreate any instrument you might want, without needing loads of storage space.

Get Recording!

Now you've got everything, go nuts! The best way to learn is to do — start making songs and follow in Billie's footsteps by uploading them to sites such as Soundcloud. We'll see you on tour!

AWARDS AND WORLD RECORDS

BILLIE'S FANS KNOW THATSHE IS AN AMAZING WRITER AND INCREDIBLE PERFORMER, SO IT SHOULD COME AS NO SURPRISE THAT SHE'S ALREADY SCOOPED LOADS OF AWARDS AND BROKEN WORLD RECORDS. BETWEEN 2018 AND 2020 BILLIE WAS NOMINATED FOR MORE THAN 100 AWARDS AND WON 45 OF THEM! HOPE SHE'S GOT A BIG TROPHY CABINET AT HOME.

THE GRAMMYS

The Grammys are the biggest awards in American music, and at the 2020 Grammys Billie took home five of the six awards she was nominated for. That included all four of the event's main prizes for Album of the Year, Best Pop Vocal Album, Record of the Year and Song of the Year. She was also named Best New Artist — as if there was any doubt! She is the first teenager in history to win all four of the top Grammys.

AND SHE KEPT ON WINNING!

Billie was also named best International Female Solo Artist at the Brit Awards and won Global Artist of the Year, Songwriter of the Year and Album of the Year at the Apple Music Awards.

In 2019, she was named Best New Artist at both the American and European MTV Music Awards.

WORLD RECORDS

As well as industry awards, Billie is a world record breaker too. She holds the Guinness World Record for being the youngest female artist in history to reach the top of the UK albums chart, a feat she accomplished when she was only 17 years and 114 days old!

Billie will also go down in history as the first artist born in the 21st century to have a chart-topping album on the Billboard 200 in the USA.

With the release of *No Time To Die*, Billie became the youngest artist ever to record a James Bond theme song.

To cap off her amazing achievements, Billie holds the world record for having the most singles on the Billboard Hot 100 chart at the same time. In April 2019 she had a whopping 14 songs on the chart! Save some room for everyone else, Billie!

CLASSIC BILLIE!

BILLIE HAS NEVER BEEN SHY ABOUT SHARING HER REACTIONS AND OPINIONS AND OFTEN USES HER CELEBRITY STATUS TO PROMOTE THINGS SHE BELIEVES IN. HERE ARE SOME OF BILLIE'S CLASSIC MOMENTS.

BILLIE VS NYLON MAGAZINE

Billie unloaded big time on German magazine *NYLON* after they made her their cover star. Why would a celeb be angry about being on a magazine cover? Because they got an artist to draw Billie as a weird, bald, naked robot and didn't even ask her permission. Billie famously wears baggy clothes because she doesn't want people talking about her body so you can bet she was unimpressed with this creepy tribute!

'You're gonna make a picture of me shirtless?' she wrote on Instagram. 'That's not real?? At 17? And make it the cover????' The magazine apologised and took the cover offline rather than face the wrath of Billie!

BILLIE VS CLIMATE CHANGE

Billie has often spoken out about the need to tackle climate change and other environmental issues. She goes further than just talking about it though. In November 2019 she teamed up with activist group Global Citizen to encourage her fans to sign up and take action against poverty, inequality and climate change. Everyone who signed up to take part in climate change protests was entered into a draw to win free tickets to her sold-out tour — where every concert had strict recycling policies and featured an 'eco-village' where fans could learn more about green issues. Helping to save the world while being an awesome pop star? Classic Billie!

BILLIE DANCES WITH FANS

It wasn't so long ago that Billie was just another teenager, idolising her fave pop stars. Now she's the fave pop star of millions of people, and she knows how to pay it back. A classic example came when the video game *Just Dance 2020* added Billie's *bad guy* to its track listing. A bunch of Billie fans were invited into a studio thinking they were just going to help test the game. Little did they know that Billie herself was on the set, watching them. When she sneaked up behind them and started dancing along, their reactions were amazing!

BILLIE VS VAN HALEN [WHO?]

When American talk show host Jimmy Kimmel asked Billie to name any member of the rock group Van Halen, the fact that she had no idea who they were set off an Internet firestorm as sad old men everywhere were furious about her ignorance of 80s guitar idols. The fact that the band, fond of big hair and glittery pants, haven't released an album or toured since 2012 didn't seem to matter. In the end, it was Wolfgang Van Halen — son of the group's lead guitarist Eddie Van Halen — who calmed things down, tweeting:

'If you haven't heard of Billie Eilish, go check her out. She's cool. Listen to what you want and don't shame others for not knowing what you like.'

BILLIE'S OSCAR MEME FACE

The 2020 Academy Awards were a big deal for Billie, as she took to the stage in front of Hollywood's finest to sing a cover version of *Yesterday* by The Beatles. Before that happened, however, she was already becoming Internet famous for something very different. The show's hosts, comedy actors Maya Rudolph and Kristen Wiig, sang a medley of Oscar-winning songs, and as they strained to hit a particularly high note from the song *Lady in Red*, the live TV cameras cut to Billie, whose horrified expression immediately trended online. Don't blame you, Billie!

ILLIE DOES BOND!

E'S *NO TIME TO DIE* PUTS HER IN AN ELITE
UP OF SINGERS WHO HAVE PROVIDED THE
ME TUNE TO JAMES BOND MOVIES.

HOOSING BILLIE

e first James Bond movie, *Dr. No*,
me out more than half a century ago
1962! Since then there have been 25
ms starring the stylish secret agent
nd recording a theme song for his
dventures is considered a huge honour.
The film's producer, Barbara Broccoli,
lew to meet Billie and Finneas after a
concert in Dublin and personally asked
them to try writing a song for *No Time To Die*, the latest Bond movie.

Billie wasn't the only singer asked to record a potential theme song. It was up to the film's composer, Hans Zimmer, to pick the one he liked best. Zimmer won't say who else tried to get the job, but he says he couldn't get past the intro of most offerings! But then he heard Billie. 'That's the vibe,' he says. 'It's a perfect movie song.'

RECORDING *NO TIME TO DIE*

Billie recorded her vocals for the song on the bed on her tour bus. Finneas claims that if you were to take away all the instruments, you'd be able to hear cleaners vacuuming outside!

Billie and Finneas then flew to London to work on the music with Zimmer and a 70-piece orchestra. Finneas and Zimmer would fill their free time by improvising piano duets with each other.

The guitar parts on the song were recorded by Johnny Marr, who was a member of famous 1980s indie band The Smiths.

The song went to the top of the charts in Britain, giving Billie her first ever UK number one!

FUN FACTS

Other stars who have recorded Bond themes include Adele, Sam Smith, Madonna and Alicia Keys.

Hans Zimmer also wrote the music for *The Dark Knight* series of Batman movies, as well the *Pirates of the Caribbean* films.

'It feels crazy to be a part of this in every way,' Billie says. 'To be able to score the theme song to a film that is part of such a legendary series is a huge honour. James Bond is the coolest film franchise ever to exist. I'm still in shock.'

CELEBRITY STANS

BILLIE'S SUCCESS HAS MADE WAVES ACROSS THE WORLD, MEANING THAT SHE HAS SOME PRETTY MAJOR CELEBRITY ADMIRERS. HERE ARE JUST A FEW OF THE STARS WHO ARE OUT-AND-PROUD BILLIE FANS!

JUSTIN BIEBER

Billie was a huge Belieber when she was younger and was blown away when her idol Justin Bieber finally followed her back on social media. The pair went on to work together on a new version of *bad guy*, while Justin cried talking about their friendship in an interview.

'I don't want her to lose it, I don't want her to go through anything I went through.' He let Billie know that 'If she ever needs me, I'm just a call away.'

ELTON JOHN

The 1970s pop titan Elton John, whose life story was turned into the hit movie *Rocketman*, says that Billie is:

'One of the most talented young ladies I've ever heard' and that her album is 'amazing'. Elton later interviewed Billie for his *Beats 1* radio show.

'She has something very special going on,' he reckons.

> **One of the most talented young ladies I've ever heard.**

DAVE GROHL

Originally the drummer for legendary grunge band Nirvana, and now the driving force behind stadium rock legends Foo Fighters, Dave Grohl has revealed similarities between Billie and Nirvana.

'The same thing is happening with her that happened with Nirvana in 1991. When I look at someone like Billie Eilish, rock 'n' roll is not even close to being dead', Dave Grohl told a music industry conference.

JULIA ROBERTS

Julia Roberts, one of the highest paid movie stars in the world and the star of *Pretty Woman*, said in an interview that:

'Billie Eilish is everything'. When she met Billie in 2018, Julia posted an excited selfie of them both to her Instagram, declaring 'I heart Billie Eilish'.

THOM YORKE

The lead singer of arty adult rock band Radiohead, Thom Yorke, took his daughter to a Billie concert in London and later told *The Times* newspaper that:

'She's doing her own thing. Nobody's telling her what to do'. Yorke met Billie backstage and told her that she was 'the only one doing anything interesting' in pop music.

COLLABORATORS

THE POP WORLD IS FULL OF COLLABORATIONS. HERE ARE SOME OF THE MOST NOTABLE PEOPLE BILLIE HAS TEAMED UP WITH.

KHALID

Billie's most high profile collab was with Khalid on the song *lovely*. Like Billie, Khalid first found fame on Soundcloud before being signed. He and Billie were friends for several years before recording *lovely* together for the soundtrack to *13 Reasons Why*.

'From the moment I heard her voice, I knew she was gonna be a star,' he told Ellen Degeneres in 2020.

ALICIA KEYS

The mutual admiration between Billie and R & B superstar Alicia went back and forth on social media for a while before they finally met on *The Late Late Show with James Corden*. Billie showed a pre-fame home video of her singing Alicia's song *Fallin* before the pair took to the stage together for a stunning duet version of *ocean eyes*.

'I'm a super, super fan of yours,' Alicia told Billie. 'I love how you write. I love your music.'

JUSTIN BIEBER

Another artist that Billie loved as a kid who has since turned into a creative partner, Justin Bieber was thrilled to lend his voice to an exclusive remix of *bad guy* in 2019. The cover art to the single featured a young Billie, posing in front of her bedroom wall covered in Bieber posters!

BTS

This one hasn't happened — yet — but that hasn't stopped members of the world-famous Korean boy band from saying they'd love to work on a track with Billie. The band, who have sold more than 40 million albums worldwide, have worked with Halsey and Nicki Minaj so another USA crossover would definitely be their style. Will it happen? Maybe not...

BILLIE DOESN'T LIKE COLLABORATIONS!

Despite several big musical team-ups, Billie isn't a fan of collaborations and doesn't really want to do any more.

'I don't like working with other people,' she told *Spin* magazine. 'I get really in my head and weird. I don't like mixing friendships with music for some reason. I don't even play songs for my friends until they're fully done.

I don't like people watching me work... and I'm doing pretty well on my own, so I'm OK.'

She does have a secret list of 'three or four' artists that she would break her rule for, though, so we may yet hear a few Billie duets in the future...

BILLIE THE FUTURE?

BILLIE HAS DONE A LOT IN ONLY A FEW YEARS, BUT WHERE DOES SHE GO FROM HERE? CHECK OUT THESE PREDICTIONS…

MAKING MUSIC? PROBABILITY: 10/10

Well, duh. Of course, Billie is going to keep making music, and she and Finneas are already working on her second album, but don't believe online rumours about it being ready right now. In January 2020 she told *iHeart Radio*:

'This year, no, but I will be making it this year. But next few years? It's coming when it's made. It's not made yet.'

DIRECTING? PROBABILITY: 9/10

Billie has always been very visual, constantly sketching and scribbling, and she always comes up with ideas for her own videos. She knew exactly what the video for *when the party's over* would look like, and started directing for herself with the video for *xanny*. You should definitely expect her to shoot more of her own promos, and don't be surprised if she turns out a short film or two.

FASHION? PROBABILITY: 8/10

Billie has been making and customising her own clothes for years, and has worked with several fashion labels on her own merchandise ranges. She has such a unique style and a drive to create, so there's a very good chance she'll become a lot more involved in the clothing that bears her name – and could even launch her own label.

WRITING?

PROBABILITY: 4/10

Billie's songs always tell a story, and she loves creating characters. Does that mean we could see her name on the spine of a novel that she's written? Possibly! She would definitely write an amazing book, but novels take a long time to write and Billie's is pretty busy with music. But years into the future... who knows?

ACTING?

PROBABILITY: 1/10

Loads of pop stars are lured in front of the camera to try and become actors as well, but it doesn't always work out. Both her parents (and Finneas) are actors, and Billie already tried acting as a kid but absolutely hated it. It's possible that she might change her mind now she'd have more control over what she worked on, but it seems very unlikely.

WHAT SORT OF BILLIE FAN ARE YOU?

YOUR FAVE BILLIE SONGS CAN SAY A LOT ABOUT YOUR PERSONALITY. PUT TOGETHER A PLAYLIST BY CHOOSING ONE TRACK FROM EACH SECTION AND SEE WHAT KIND OF BILLIE FAN YOU ARE!

1. A) ocean eyes
   B) bad guy
   C) bellyache

2. A) wish you were gay
   B) xanny
   C) you should see me in a crown

3. A) when the party's over
   B) COPYCAT
   C) everything i wanted

4. A) lovely (with Khalid)
   B) my boy
   c) bury a friend

5. A) ilomilo
   B) come out and play
   C) listen before i go

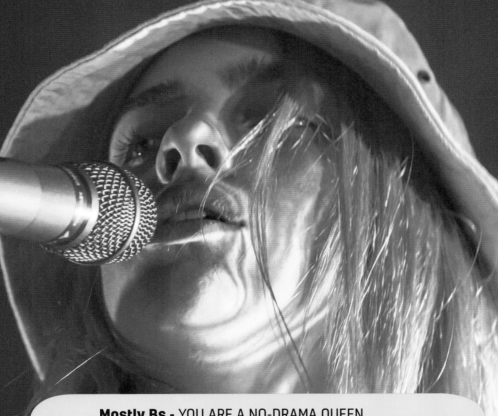

Mostly As - YOU ARE A TRAGIC ROMANTIC

You're drawn to songs about love and romance, but you definitely don't expect them to end happily. You know that relationships can lead to heartbreak and you're OK with that. In fact, there's something kind of beautiful about that aching pain.

Mostly Bs - YOU ARE A NO-DRAMA QUEEN

You prefer songs about the ways that friends and strangers behave. You're the one in your social circle who keeps up with the drama but can't even deal with it at the same time. When someone texts you with the latest gossip, you roll your eyes but read it anyway.

Mostly Cs - YOU ARE A FANTASY FIEND

You love a song that tells a story, the stranger and more twisted the better. You like exploring the darker side of your thoughts and emotions through the safety of fiction and that actually makes you a nicer, happier person!

ANSWERS

TRUE OR FALSE?
p 34-35

1. False.
2. True.
3. False.
4. True.
5. True.
6. False.
7. True.
8. True.
9. True.
10. False.

11. True.
12. False.
13. False.
14. False.
15. True.
16. True.
17. False.
18. True.
19. True.
20. False.

21. True.
22. True.
23. True.
24. False.
25. False.
26. False
27. True
28. False

HOW WELL DO YOU KNOW BILLIE?

p 48-49

1. Highland Park.

2. Sagittarius.

3. *Iron Man.*

4. A black hole.

5. 1997.

6. *fingers crossed*

7. Horse.

8. The Slightlys.

9. For a dance class.

10. Soundcloud.

11. She swallowed an ant by mistake.

12. Khalid.

13. wherearetheavocados.

14. Alistair.

15. *!!!!!!!*

16. *Sherlock.*

17. Tourette's syndrome.

18. *Bored.*

19. *Yesterday* by The Beatles.

20. The *Don't Smile At Me* tour.

21. *bad guy*

22. *No Time To Die*

23. In a treehouse in her back garden.

24. A spider.

25. *ilomilo*

26. *X-Men Apocalypse.*

27. Synaesthesia.

28. Fourteen.

LYRIC QUIZ
p 64-65

1. *party favor.*

2. *all the good girls go to hell.*

3. *b*****es broken hearts.*

4. *lovely (with Khalid).*

5. *Bored.*

6. *when the party's over.*

7. *my strange addiction.*

8. *bury a friend.*

9. *Fingers Crossed.*

10. *everything i wanted.*

11. *listen before i go.*

12. *xanny.*

13. *bellyache.*

14. *COPYCAT.*

15. *my boy.*

16. *ocean eyes.*

17. *watch.*

18. *No Time To Die.*

19. *bad guy.*

20. *you should see me in a crown.*

PICTURE CREDITS

The publisher would like to thank the following for permission to reproduce their images:
(t = top, b = bottom, l = left, r = right, c = centre)

Cover
(c) © Ben Houdijk / Shutterstock.com; (br) © DFree / Shutterstock.com.

Alamy
40(cl) © WENN Rights Ltd; 50(bl) © Tilman Jentzsch / Gonzales Photo; 52-53(c) © Jason Richardson; 53(tr) © dpa picture alliance 57(c) © MediaPunch; 59(tr) © Guy Bell; 60(bl) © dpa picture alliance; 61(tr) © ZUMA Press, Inc.; 62(bl) © Stian S. Moller/Gonzales Photo; 63(c) © MediaPunch Inc; 65(b) © Lasse Lagoni/Gonzales Photo; 68-69(c) © Tilman Jentzsch/Gonzales Photo; 71(c) © Image Press Agency; 74-75(c) © UPI; 77(c) © Andie Mills; 80bl © Andie Mills; 87(c) © ZUMA Press, Inc; 89(c) © Andie Mills; 93(c) © Christian Bertrand.

Getty Images
18-19 (l & r) © Kevin Mazur; 25br © Mat Hayward; 37(c) © Amy Sussman; 38(c) © Samir Hussain/WireImage; 39(c) © Presley Ann/WireImage; 41(c) © Emma McIntyre/Getty Images for Spotify; 54(c) © Kevin Winter.

Shutterstock
06(tl) © Ben Houdijk; 08(bl) © DFree; 10-11(c) © Nomad_Soul; 12(tl) © canyalcin; 14l(c) © Artography; (c) © Christian Bertrand; 15(tr) © Liv Oeian; 16-17(c) © Christian Bertland; © Canyalcin; © Ned Snowman; © Christian Bertrand; © DFree; © DFree; © Christian Bertrand; © Ben Houdijk; © Canyalcin; © Liv Oeian; © Ned Snowman; © Christian Bertrand; © Trekandshoot; 20-21(c) © Christian Bertrand; 22(cl) © Featureflash Photo Agency; 23(cl) © Tinseltown; 24 © Ben Houdijk; 26-27(c) © Christian Bertrand; 28-29(c) © Ben Houdijk; 30-31(c) © Ben Houdijk; 34-35(c) © DFree; 38(c) © Joe Seer; 42(c) © Tinseltown; 46(tl) © Nataliya Arzamasova; 51(c) © Ben Houdijk; 55(br) © Christian Bertrand; 66(cl) © agwilson; (br) © Frederic Legrand – COMEO; 67(c) © Christian Bertrand; (tl) © Lenscap Photography; (bl) © Featureflash Photo Agency; (br) © Thomas Quack; 80-81(c) © LeStudio.

Other
24(tl) © Billie Eilish/Instagram; 43(c) © H&M publicity; 44-45 (l & r) © eOne; © AMC; © NBC; © Studiocanal; 79(c) © Billboard.

All other images, including emoticons and miscellaneous objects courtesy of Shutterstock.com.

REFERENCES

9: BBC, 'Billie Eilish: Is she pop's best new hope?'
[www.bbc.co.uk/news/entertainment-arts-40580489]

10-11, 13 & 36: NME, 'The Big Read – Billie Eilish: the most talked-about teen on the planet'
[www.nme.com/big-reads/big-read-billie-eilish-interview-nme-100-2019-2425970]

12: Rolling Stone, 'BILLIE EILISH And the Triumph of the Weird'
[www.rollingstone.com/music/music-features/billie-eilish-cover-story-triumph-weird-863603/]

13: Interview Magazine, 'DISCOVERY: BILLIE EILISH'
[www.interviewmagazine.com/music/discovery-billie-eilish]

24: NARCITY, 'Billie Eilish 'Social Distances' With Cute Puppies From Los Angeles Rescue'
[www.narcity.com/gossip/us/ca/los-angeles/billie-eilishs-instagram-story-shows-her-social-distancing-with-adorable-puppies]

25: Variety, 'Billie Eilish Talks Depression, Fan Empathy, Soundcloud and Spiders at Grammy Museum' [https://variety.com/2019/music/news/billie-eilish-grammy-museum-1203340928/]

26 & 27: The Fader, 'Who's Billie Eilish?' [www.thefader.com/2019/03/05/billie-eilish-cover-story]

28 & 29: iHeart Radio, 'Billie Eilish Explains How Synaesthesia Affects Her Music'
[www.iheart.com/content/2019-05-29-billie-eilish-explains-how-synesthesia-affects-her-music/]

30 & 31: Milk.xyz, 'Billie Eilish on Homeschooling, Humility & Overnight Success'
[https://milk.xyz/articles/billie-eilish-on-homeschooling-humility-overnight-success/]

44: AltPress, 'Billie Eilish credits cult horror flick as 'main inspiration' for album art'
[https://www.altpress.com/news/billie-eilish-the-babadook-inspiration/] Bazaar, 'Billie Eilish is a 15-year-old pop prodigy – and she's intimidating as hell' [www.harpersbazaar.com/culture/art-books-music/a13040159/billie-eilish-interview/]

45: MTV, 'Billie Eilish tells us about her Spotify pop-up, sampling The Office, and ending her album with 'An R.I.P' [www.mtv.com/news/3118812/inside-billie-eilish-experience-spotify/] PBN, 'Billie Eilish Reveals Her Vegan Taco Bell Burrito Order' [www.plantbasednews.org/news/billie-eilish-20-vegan-burritos-taco-bell] YouTube, Noisey, 'Billie Eilish Talks Her Love for Anime While Drawing Her Self-Portrait' [www.youtube.com watch?v=4HmFgsLjpnM]

58: NME, 'Billie Eilish explains what 'Bad Guy' is about' [www.nme.com/news/music/billie-eilish-breaks-down-bad-guy-lyrics-2543500] The Guardian, 'Billie Eilish: the pop icon who defines 21st-century teenage angst' [www.theguardian.com/music/2019/mar/29/billie-eilish-the-pop-icon-who-defines-21st-century-teenage-angst]

59: coup de main, 'Interview + Photo Diary: Billie Eilish x Laneway 2018'
[www.coupdemainmagazine.com/billie-eilish/13987]

60: Billboard, 'Billie Eilish Explains How 'You Should See In A Crown' Was Inspired by BBC's 'Sherlock'' [www.billboard.com/articles/columns/pop/8483538/billie-eilish-video-interview-you-should-see-me-in-a-crown] Genius, 'Billie Eilish Breaks Down 'COPYCAT' On Genius' Series 'Verified''[https://genius.com/a/billie-eilish-breaks-down-copycat-on-genius-series-verified]

61: COSMOPOLITAN, 'Billie Eilish Has an Intense Nightmare in Her New Song, 'Everything I Wanted'
[www.cosmopolitan.com/entertainment/music/a29800237/billie-eilish-song-everything-i-wanted-lyrics-explained/] POP BUZZ, 'Billie Eilish responds to the 'wish you were gay' backlash' [https://www.popbuzz.com/music/news/billie-eilish-wish-you-were-gay-backlash/

62: YouTube, First We Feast, 'Billie Eilish Freaks Out While Eating Spicy Wings |Hot Ones' [www.youtube.com/watch?v=YDr4lTrp7YI]

63: YouTube, Genius, 'Billie Eilish 'idontwannabeyouanymore' Official Lyrics & Meaning | Verified' [www. youtube.com/watch?v=-BzvCCzH-n0] Rolling Stone, 'Billie Eilish's Teenage Truths' [www.rollingstone. com/music/music-features/billie-eilish-album-songs-interview-tour-tickets-797040/]

67 & 69: CLASH, 'Don't Wanna Be You: Billie Eilish Interviewed' [https://www.clashmusic.com/ features/dont-wanna-be-you-billie-eilish-interviewed]

68: ELLE, '15-Year-Old Music Prodigy Billie Eilish On Influences, Inspiration And What She's Listening to RN' [www.elle.com.au/culture/billie-eilish-interview-playlist-influences-inspiration-14756]

69: Atwood Magazine, 'Wholehearted Obsession: A conversation with Finneas' [https:// atwoodmagazine.com/finneas-2018-interview/]

71: Ones to Watch, 'Finneas Debuts 'I'm In Love Without You' & Poloroid Gallery by Billie Eilish' [www.onestowatch.com/blog/premiere-qa-finneas-debuts-im-in-love]

76: BBC, 'Billie Eilish offended by cyborg magazine cover' [www.bbc.co.uk/news/entertainment-arts-49509496]

77: Global Citizen, '6 Times Billie Eilish Spoke Out Against the Climate Crisis' [www.globalcitizen.org/en/content/what-has-billie-eilish-said-about-climate-change/]

78: YouTube, Just Dance, 'Billie Eilish Suprises Her Biggest Fans | Just Dance 2020' [www.youtube.com/watch?v=uyyQlWNesGM] National Post, 'Billie Eilish doesn't know who Van Halen is, but why do we even care?' [https://nationalpost.com/entertainment/music/billie-eilish-doesnt-know-who-van-halen-is-but-why-do-we-even-care]

79: Billboard, Billie Eilish's Face Won the Oscar for Best Reaction Shot' [www.billboard.com/articles/ news/awards/8550545/billie-eilish-face-oscars-2020-reaction-memes]

80 & 81: 007, 'Billie Eilish to Perform No Time to Die title song' [www.007.com/billie-eilish-announced-for-no-time-to-die-title-song/]

007, 'No Time to Die UK Number One' [www.007.com/no-time-to-die-uk-number-one/] Vulture, 'The Girl With the Midas Touch' [www.vulture.com/2020/03/billie-eilish-interview-james-bond-theme-hans-zimmer.html]

82 & 83: NME, 'Billie Eilish – Album Of The Year: 2019 was hers' [www.nme.com/big-reads/billie-eilish-album-of-the-year-2019-was-hers-2587038] Billboard, 'A Timeline of Justin Bieber & Billie Eilish's Dream-Come-True Friendship'[www.billboard.com/articles/columns/pop/8551534/justin-bieber-billie-eilish-friendship-timeline] NME, 'Elton John on Billie Eilish: 'Talent like hers doesn't come along very often'[www.nme.com/news/music/elton-john-on-billie-eilish-talent-like-hers-doesnt-come-along-very-often-2521214] Refinery29, 'Julia Roberts Explains Her Obsession With Billie Eilish' [www.refinery29. com/en-us/2018/12/218716/julia-roberts-billie-eilish-friendship-instagram] The Times, 'Thom Yorke interview: the Radiohead frontman on his new solo album, Anima, why he struggles if he can't make music, and Billie Eilish' [www.thetimes.co.uk/article/thom-yorke-interview-radiohead-anima-billie-eilish-2wnwqmxdw]

84 & 85: Billboard, 'This Is the Moment Khalid Knew Billie Eilish Was 'Gonna Be a Star' [www.billboard.com/articles/news/9327513/khalid-ellen-interview-billie-eilish] Showbiz Cheat Sheet, 'Alicia Keys Opens up About the 'Real Special' Connection She Has With Billie Eilish' [www. cheatsheet.com/entertainment/alicia-keys-opens-up-about-the-real-special-connection-she-has-with-billie-eilish.html/] NME, 'BTS hint that a collaboration with Billie Eilish is on the way' [www.nme.com/ news/music/bts-hint-that-a-collaboration-with-billie-eilish-is-on-the-way-2584953]